A BLUE BANNER
BIOGRAPHY

Jessica Simpson

Michelle Medlock Adams

P.O. Box 196
Hockessin, Delaware 19707
Visit us on the web: www.mitchelllane.com
Comments? email us: mitchelllane@mitchelllane.com

Mitchell Lane PUBLISHERS

Printing   1   2   3   4   5   6   7   8   9

Blue Banner Biographies

Akon	Alan Jackson	Alicia Keys
Allen Iverson	Ashanti	Ashlee Simpson
Ashton Kutcher	Avril Lavigne	Bernie Mac
Beyoncé	Bow Wow	Britney Spears
Carrie Underwood	Chris Brown	Chris Daughtry
Christina Aguilera	Christopher Paul Curtis	Ciara
Clay Aiken	Condoleezza Rice	Daniel Radcliffe
David Ortiz	Derek Jeter	Eminem
Eve	Fergie (Stacy Ferguson)	50 Cent
Gwen Stefani	Ice Cube	Jamie Foxx
Ja Rule	Jay-Z	Jennifer Lopez
Jessica Simpson	J. K. Rowling	Johnny Depp
JoJo	Justin Berfield	Justin Timberlake
Kate Hudson	Keith Urban	Kelly Clarkson
Kenny Chesney	Lance Armstrong	Lindsay Lohan
Mariah Carey	Mario	Mary J. Blige
Mary-Kate and Ashley Olsen	Michael Jackson	Miguel Tejada
Missy Elliott	Nancy Pelosi	Nelly
Orlando Bloom	P. Diddy	Paris Hilton
Peyton Manning	Queen Latifah	Ron Howard
Rudy Giuliani	Sally Field	Selena
Shakira	Shirley Temple	Tim McGraw
Usher	Zac Efron	

Library of Congress Cataloging-in-Publication Data
Adams, Michelle Medlock.
    Jessica Simpson / by Michelle Medlock Adams.
       p. cm. — (Blue banner biographies)
    Includes bibliographical references, discography (p.   ), filmography (p.   ), and index.
    ISBN 978-1-58415-616-1 (library bound)
    1. Simpson, Jessica—Juvenile literature. 2. Singers—United States—Biography—Juvenile literature. I. Title.
ML3930.S57A33 2008
782.42164092—dc22
[B]   2007019681

ABOUT THE AUTHOR: Michelle Medlock Adams is an award-winning journalist and author of 34 books, earning top honors from the Associated Press, the Society of Professional Journalists, the Sunday and Features Editors, and the Hoosier State Press Association. Her Christian living book, *Living the Love Chapter,* earned her the title of Writer of the Year in 2001 at the Write-to-Publish Conference in Wheaton, Illinois. She is also the director of Write On! The Southern Indiana Writers' Conference. She resides in Bedford, Indiana, with her husband, two tween-age daughters, and three miniature longhaired dachshunds.
PHOTO CREDITS: Cover—Gregg DeGuire/WireImage; p. 4—Kevin Mazur/WireImage; p. 7—Haraz N. Ghanbari/AP Photo; p. 12—Matt Sayles/AP Photo; p. 15—Mark Mainz/Getty Images; p. 17—PHOTOG/IPOL/Globe Photos; p. 19—Arnaldo Magnani/Getty Images; p. 23—Chicken of the Sea.
ACKNOWLEDGMENTS: The following story has been thoroughly researched and to the best of our knowledge represents a true story. While every possible effort has been made to ensure accuracy, the publisher will not assume liability for damages caused by inaccuracies in the data, and makes no warranty on the accuracy of the information contained herein. This story has not been authorized or endorsed by Jessica Simpson.

CONTENTS

Growing up in Richardson, Texas, Jessica Simpson always had dreams of sharing her voice with the world. Today, she is living that dream. Her gorgeous smile and angelic voice have taken her to A-list celebrity status and made her America's sweetheart.

A Reason to Smile

*T*wenty-five-year-old Jessica Simpson, known for her angelic voice and stunning beauty, was a world away from the glitz and glamour of Hollywood this October day in 2005. Instead of a chauffeured limousine, Jessica rode in a dusty bus through western Kenya, Africa, from Nairobi to Nakuru.

Her destination? An Operation Smile medical clinic, where a team of medical professionals was ready to begin the day's facial reconstructive surgeries on dozens of children. Operation Smile is a private, nonprofit volunteer medical services organization that provides free reconstructive surgery and related healthcare to children around the world who suffer from facial deformities.

Though Jessica had served as Operation Smile's International Youth Ambassador since 2003, she had never experienced a day like this. With her long blond hair tied back in a bandana, Jessica helped the volunteer team with the medical evaluations of 280 patients who came into the clinic that day. She kept the children company while they waited to see the doctors. She found ways to make the kids smile, giving them gifts, laughing with them, and loving them.

During those hours, Jessica became quite fond of an eighteen-month-old little girl named Boke, who desperately needed surgery to correct a facial deformity. Boke's father wanted to give his little daughter a chance at a normal life and was willing to do anything he could to make that happen. He had sold one of his six cows to get money and traveled twelve hours to the clinic in Nakuru, hoping Boke would get the needed surgery. The father's devotion to his daughter had paid off. The doctors agreed to treat her.

As Boke was prepped for surgery, Jessica comforted the child and stayed with her throughout the entire operation.

"I was there from scrub-up to the end," Jessica said in an article for *Entertainment News* on AOL.

After Boke's surgery and recovery, Jessica hugged little Boke awhile before handing her back to her father. Being a part of such important and meaningful work that week really touched Jessica's heart.

"My experience in Kenya with Operation Smile was incredible," she shared in an Operation Smile press release on March 16, 2006. "To witness the truly miraculous

> *Being a part of such important and meaningful work that week really touched Jessica's heart.*

transformations in the lives of so many desperate needy children was both powerful and personally rewarding."

Jessica's husband at the time, singer Nick Lachey (luh-SHAY), usually accompanied Jessica on Operation Smile trips, but Nick wasn't with Jessica in Africa. Instead, Jessica was accompanied by her manager and father, Joe Simpson; her friend and hairstylist, Ken Paves; and her friend Cacee Cobb. This seemed especially strange since it was Jessica and Nick's third wedding anniversary.

Tabloids and web sites had been saying the same thing for quite some time: "Jessica and Nick's marriage is in trouble." The couple denied those reports over and over again. However, Nick's absence in Africa spoke quite loudly. Only one month later, Jessica and Nick announced their official separation with this statement: "After three

Jessica shares a moment with Dr. Bill Magee, Jr. Dr. Magee is the CEO and cofounder of Operation Smile, which is a nonprofit, private volunteer medical services organization. It provides free reconstructive surgery for children with facial deformities.

years of marriage and careful thought and consideration, we have decided to part ways. This is the mutual decision of two people with an enormous amount of respect and admiration for each other. We hope that you respect our privacy during this difficult time."

> **"I was in hospitals with all these sick kids. . . . I just knew I needed to find something more in my life, on my own."**

Jessica was quoted in *Jane* magazine as saying, "I went there on our three-year wedding anniversary. He stayed home." She said she realized then that her marriage to Nick was over. That trip to Kenya changed her life.

"On that day, everything became so clear," she shared. "I was in hospitals with all these sick kids. . . . I just knew I needed to find something more in my life, on my own."

With her willing heart, Jessica had given the children of Africa a reason to smile that week. She just hoped she could find a reason to smile again when she began her new life — without Nick.

America's Sweetheart

Joe and Tina Simpson welcomed their first child, Jessica Ann, into the world on July 10, 1980, in Dallas, Texas. Joe Truett Simpson, a Baptist youth minister and adolescent therapist, and Tina Ann (Drew) Simpson, a Sunday school teacher and aerobics instructor, couldn't have been happier with their healthy, beautiful baby girl. Like most parents, they had high hopes for her, but they had no idea their little sweetie would someday become America's sweetheart and one of its most famous newlyweds.

Just when the Simpson family thought they couldn't get any happier, they welcomed baby Ashlee on October 3, 1984. Jessica loved having a little sister. The family of four filled their lives with faith, love, laughter, and lots of singing.

The girls grew up outside of Dallas in a city called Richardson. From the very beginning, God played a big part in their lives. Jessica spent many hours at church, playing and singing and enjoying life. Joe noticed that Jessica's voice had a certain angelic quality to it, and he began encouraging her to sing during the Baptist church services. She sang in the choir and eventually belted out solos for the congregation.

By age twelve, Jessica was becoming more confident in her voice and less nervous about performing in front of large groups. When tryouts for *The All New Mickey Mouse Club* came to Dallas, Jessica went after her dreams. Not surprisingly, she wasn't the only one who wanted a coveted spot on the show. In fact, she was one of about 30,000 young performers trying out across the country, including future Mouseketeers and pop stars Britney Spears, Christina Aguilera, and Justin Timberlake. Jessica advanced in the competition and was invited to Florida to participate in a two-week audition to showcase her dancing, singing, and acting skills. However, as the tryout process continued, Jessica's nerves got the best of her. When it was her turn to wow the judges, Jessica couldn't remember the words to her song and forgot some of the dance steps. While the producers felt she had talent, Jessica wasn't chosen to be on the show.

> *When tryouts for The All New Mickey Mouse Club came to Dallas, Jessica went after her dreams.*

"I wanted to give up, but my family kept me going," Jessica once said when asked about the auditions.

Her career really began two years later while singing at a summer church camp. Buster Soaries, the head of a small contemporary Christian record label, heard Jessica sing "Amazing Grace" and knew immediately that he had discovered a Texas treasure. The blond beauty began working on her album, but after three years, the small record label went out of business before the album could be finished and released.

Of course she was disappointed, but Jessica's family never let her give up on her dream of becoming a professional singer. While attending J. J. Pearce High School in Richardson, she found time to take vocal lessons and continue improving on her talent. She also enjoyed typical high school activities, like being the head cheerleader and being crowned homecoming queen twice. She attracted the attention of many boys, but she was very clear in her beliefs. She didn't want to have sex before marriage, and she stood strong in her faith even though other girls her age were living the wild life.

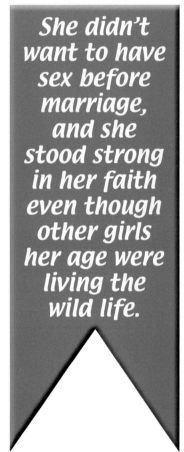

She didn't want to have sex before marriage, and she stood strong in her faith even though other girls her age were living the wild life.

"My first kiss was when I was fourteen," she said in an interview featured on IMDb.com. "I could tell it was coming because Jason picked up a handful of mints. We

Joe (Jessica's dad), Jessica, Nick (Jessica's husband at the time), Tina (Jessica's mom), and Ashlee (Jessica's sister) celebrate the opening of the 2005 blockbuster movie, Dukes of Hazzard, *in which Jessica starred as Daisy Duke. Jessica worked out hard and restricted her diet prior to the filming of the movie so that she could look great in those famous short jean shorts that the original Daisy Duke wore in the television series.*

had been going out for over a year, so it was really special."

Jessica's foundation of faith and family would prove especially important as her career exploded—and that was about to happen.

From Gospel Girl to Pop Princess

Since the record label she'd signed with had gone under before her project could be completed, Jessica wondered if she'd ever have a CD of her own. Then her grandma, Joyce, had a surprise for her. She gave Jessica the money to finish her CD. That's how much she believed in her granddaughter's ability. In fact, the whole family felt that way. They knew Jessica's talent was rare and ready to be shared with the world.

So, with a completed CD in hand, Jessica dropped out of high school her senior year to pursue her music career. (She later received her GED.) Jessica began touring the Christian youth conference circuit with her father, Joe. He preached and she sang songs like "True Love Waits," and after each service they sold copies of her CD. Sometimes she would perform in front of 20,000 people, sharing the stage with Christian contemporary music stars Kirk Franklin, God's Property, and CeCe Winans. Jessica ended up selling every single copy of her CD.

One of those CDs made its way to the hands of Tommy Mottola of Columbia Records, and he liked what he heard. He believed he could make her into a pop star, so he signed her to a recording contract. The little girl with a voice that floated up and down five octaves was on her way to stardom!

Jessica's faith was important to her, and she didn't want her move to secular music to compromise what she believed. Mr. Mottola respected her beliefs and said that Columbia would support her values. It was August of 1997, and Jessica's career was heating up as hot as the Texas summer.

By the time Jessica signed with Columbia Records, she was a gorgeous seventeen-year-old who could sing a ballad with more poise and passion than stars twice her age. Mr. Mottola knew that and decided Jessica should wow her new pop audience with some strong ballads. Jessica was totally in agreement with that decision. She wanted to set herself apart from the other pop princesses who were climbing the charts — Britney Spears and Christina Aguilera. She was quoted as saying, "I want people to fall in love with my voice before my image."

That's what she set out to do — but along the way, she fell in love.

In December 1998, at the Hollywood Christmas Parade in Los Angeles, Jessica met Nick Lachey of the popular boy band 98 Degrees. Nick has said in several interviews that it was love at first sight as he watched her sing and the crowd react to her. She was also interested in him. There was chemistry right from the beginning. In an interview with Ryan Seacrest on CNN's *Larry King Live*, Jessica said that after seeing Nick at the parade, she told her parents, "He is the guy I want to marry."

The two met again at a party given by *Teen People* magazine. Nick was there with his mother, and he told her, "Mom, I really kind of like this girl, and your job, your assignment for the night, is to get me in good with this girl."

Nick's mom took her assignment seriously. She let Jessica know that Nick was no longer dating anyone. Jessica got the message loud and clear, and she was secretly thrilled to hear the news of Nick's availability.

To Jessica's and Nick's delight, Jessica was booked to open for 98 Degrees for the band's Heat It Up concert tour in 1999. The tour gave the twosome a lot of time to talk

Jessica and Nick fell quickly for each other. They met in December 1998 at the Hollywood Christmas Parade in Los Angeles. Shortly after meeting Nick, Jessica told her parents, "He is the guy I want to marry." Luckily, Nick said it was practically love at first sight for him, too.

and get to know each other better. They began dating when time permitted, but Jessica was still quite young. She wasn't yet nineteen and had never really dated anyone seriously. Plus, she was committed to saving herself for her husband and abstaining from premarital sex. She knew Nick Lachey had thousands of girls throwing themselves at him at every concert, so she wasn't sure he would want to date her if he knew of her strong religious beliefs.

By mid-1999, Jessica had definitely crossed over to pop princess, but her Christian values had remained intact.

"She told me, I think, in the very first phone conversation we ever had . . . about her belief in saving herself and so I mean, she laid it out there right away . . . ," Nick told Ryan Seacrest in the *Larry King Live* interview. "I respected that."

"I had to tell him in the beginning," Jessica added.

By mid-1999, Jessica had definitely crossed over to pop princess, but her Christian values had remained intact. She had a handsome boyfriend to stand by her through the good and bad times, and the good times were only getting better.

On November 23, 1999, Jessica proudly released her debut pop album, *Sweet Kisses*, which ended up selling two million copies in the United States. Her first single, "I Wanna Love You Forever," reached the top five of the U.S. Billboard Hot 100 singles chart.

Jessica sings at a 2001 youth concert in Washington, D.C. She released an up-tempo CD, Irresistible, *in mid-2001, and it quickly climbed to number six on the Billboard 200 album chart. Jessica's career was really on fire.*

Delays, Detours, and Dreams

Not only was Jessica enjoying sweet kisses from her boyfriend, Nick, her *Sweet Kisses* album was enjoying sweet success. It went double platinum thanks to the popularity of her singles "I Think I'm in Love with You" and "Where You Are," which she sang with Nick. She also had great success with her single "Woman in Me," which featured Destiny's Child. Her song "Did You Ever Love Somebody" ended up on the soundtrack of the wildly popular TV show *Dawson's Creek.*

After the 98 Degrees tour ended, Jessica began touring with heartthrob Ricky Martin. She opened for him with her own troupe of dancers, which included her younger sister, Ashlee, who was following in her sister's famous footsteps.

Jessica's career was on fire, but it wasn't red hot like Britney's and Christina's were. They were practically household names by the beginning of 2000. The powerful people at Columbia Records decided Jessica needed to do some upbeat, fun songs on her next album in order to compete with the Britneys and Christinas of the world.

That resulted in Jessica's up-tempo release *Irresistible*, which debuted in mid-2001 at number six on the Billboard 200 album chart. The title track from that album got great radio play. It peaked at number fifteen on the Hot 100 and landed in the top ten on Billboard's Top 40 Tracks.

Jessica's career was heating up, but her love life wasn't. She and Nick had decided to "take a break" during 2001.

"I didn't ever want to regret not ever dating anybody else because Nick was . . . you know, the love of my life,

Jessica and her younger sister, Ashlee, who is also a talented actress and singer, enjoy a bit of shopping together. This dynamic duo has always been tight, helping each other through bad times and celebrating with each other during good ones. They aren't just sisters; they're best friends.

and I hadn't ever really dated anyone else," Jessica explained on *Larry King Live.*

Then the terrorist attacks of September 11 happened, and everything changed. Middle Eastern extremists hijacked four airplanes and crashed two of them into the World Trade Center in New York City and one airplane into the Pentagon in Washington, D.C. The fourth plane crashed into a field in Pennsylvania. Almost 3,000 people were killed.

The events of that day affected every single person in America, and Jessica and Nick were no different. Jessica worried about Nick, and when he called to let her know that he was okay, she realized how much she loved him.

"I wanted him to come home," she said on *Larry King Live.* "That was the worst time in my life. . . . I was really, really, really selfish, and that made me realize what I was about to lose." Their separation was over.

> *"It made me realize without him in my life, what I was missing out on . . . I had the perfect guy in front of my face."*

"We fell in love all over again," Jessica said. "Like, it made me realize without him in my life, what I was missing out on. And I was out there searching to date other guys, yet I had the perfect guy in front of my face."

Nick proposed to Jessica in a romantic setting off the coast of Hawaii in February 2002, and Jessica began planning her dream wedding.

From "I Do" to Divorce

"**W**hen I was a little girl, I often dreamed about my wedding day. The bedtime story of my childhood was *Cinderella.* Although it was a fairy tale, I knew that one day I would have my own story of love to share," Jessica wrote in her book, *I Do: Achieving Your Dream Wedding.*

When Jessica was a young girl growing up in Texas, she often wrote letters to her "dream man" in her diaries. Her mom kept all those love letters, because she knew that one day her little girl would give her Prince Charming those heartfelt writings. That's exactly what Jessica did — on her wedding day, October 26, 2002, at a lovely chapel in the hilly region just outside of Austin, Texas. Jessica presented her prince, Nick, with a framed version of a romantic letter she'd written to him entitled "To My Future Husband."

Jessica also wrote a song for her husband-to-be, "My Love," which was performed at their wedding. The lyrics reveal how much she loved Nick and couldn't wait to share a life with him.

The deepest of your love is my love
The promise of your life is my life
Wherever you go, I will follow. . . .

Always you and I
Always I'll praise the skies for you
For my love

Nick also wrote a song for Jessica, "My Everything," which was performed by 98 Degrees during the ceremony. Nick's brother and best man, Drew, sang Nick's opening part. It was the storybook ceremony that twenty-two-year-old Jessica had always dreamed of, and it was the beginning of a love story that would captivate the world.

The year 2003 would prove to be a very good one for the talented Texan. Jessica's third album, *In This Skin,* was released in August and debuted at number ten on the Billboard 200 album chart. (By April 2004, the album peaked at number two.) She and her new hubby also had their own hit on their hands.

During the summer of 2003, Jessica and Nick started sharing their private life with the whole world when MTV launched the reality show *Newlyweds: Nick & Jessica.* The show was instantly popular, drawing an average of 1.4 million viewers each episode. Cameras covered the good, bad, ugly, and funny things that happen in daily married life.

"I think the last thing we wanted to do is say, 'Oh, here we are, the perfect happy couple,'" Nick said in a *Larry King Live* interview. "When we decided to do the show, we said if there's a fight, you can't hold back from that. That's part of life, too. And that's part of being a newlywed, too, and we have to be willing to let that hang out, you know, because that's part of the experience we wanted everyone to see."

The fights, though, weren't what everyone talked about the next day. People couldn't quit talking about how funny Jessica was in her "dumb blonde" kind of way. One of the most famous segments of the show featured Jessica sitting on the couch, eating Chicken of the Sea tuna and asking Nick, "So is this, like, chicken or tuna?"

Jessica enjoys a good laugh as she poses with Chicken of the Sea president and CEO Dennis Mussell. On Jessica and Nick's Newlyweds *TV reality show, Jessica once asked Nick if Chicken of the Sea was chicken or tuna, and if it was tuna, why was it called "Chicken of the Sea"? Her funny, quirky "dumb blonde" personality on their reality show took her to household-name status overnight!*

Jessica and Nick soon became household names. They had a hit reality show, a strong marriage, and thriving music careers. Jessica won three Teen Choice Awards that year, proving that she really was America's sweetheart.

> **Following in Jessica's footsteps, Ashlee recorded her own CD, Autobiography, and starred in her own hit MTV reality show.**

She wasn't the only sweetheart in the family. Her younger sister, Ashlee, had come out from the shadow of her big sister to become a star, too. She had started by touring with Jessica as a background dancer, and was now a budding actress, singer, and star. She had a bit part in an episode of *Malcolm in the Middle* in 2001. In 2002, she landed an appearance in the comedy *The Hot Chick* and earned the role of Cecilia Smith on the hit series *7th Heaven*. What was supposed to be a seven-show deal turned into a two-season role for Ashlee, and Jessica was very proud of her sister. Both have often told the press, "We're each other's biggest fans."

Following in Jessica's footsteps, Ashlee recorded her own CD, *Autobiography*, and starred in her own hit MTV reality show, *The Ashlee Simpson Show*, which debuted in June 2004. Later that year, Jessica's Christmas CD, *Re-Joyce: The Christmas Album*, was released and eventually was certified gold, which means it sold at least 500,000 copies. The album was named in honor of Jessica's grandmother, Joyce, who years before had paid for Jessica to finish recording her first CD.

The Simpson sisters had definitely made their parents proud. While their mom helped design costumes and tutor Ashlee, who was still in school, papa Joe skillfully managed their careers. It was truly a family affair.

Still quite popular, *Newlyweds* won a People's Choice Award for Favorite Reality Show before filming the final episode. Jessica said she was relieved to have the cameras out of her home so that she and Nick could finally live like a normal married couple, but her love life was about to become messy.

Success seemed to follow Jessica everywhere. She landed a huge role playing Daisy Duke in the movie *The Dukes of Hazzard*, which debuted the summer of 2005 at the top of the U.S. box office. In fact, Jessica beat out Britney Spears for that role! Jessica also recorded "These Boots Are Made for Walkin' " for the movie's soundtrack. That song hit number fourteen on the Billboard Hot 100 and won a People's Choice Award for Favorite Song from a Movie.

With her crazy filming schedule, Jessica and Nick weren't able to see each other very often. Tabloids printed rumors about an affair between Jessica and one of her costars on the set of *Dukes of Hazzard.* The press continued printing hurtful stories about how the happy newlyweds were no longer happy. Though Jessica and Nick denied all reports that their marriage was failing, by November 2005, they just couldn't fake it anymore. The couple officially separated, and Jessica filed for divorce on December 16, stating the reason was "irreconcilable differences."

Jessica turned to her mom, dad, and sister to get her through the difficult time.

Still Standing, Still Smiling

On June 30, 2006, Jessica and Nick's divorce was finalized. Both expressed deep sadness over the end of their marriage. Jessica told Britain's *Glamour* magazine, "There are still moments that I'm so hurt I can't even breathe. . . . I love Nick with all my heart. He's still a dear friend. He's part of who I am. We grew up together. I fell in love with him when I was nineteen. That's young."

While Nick appeared to rebound a bit more quickly by dating MTV's Vanessa Minnillo for most of 2006, Jessica stayed busy with work. She hosted the Teen Choice Awards in August, appeared on *The View* in September, and celebrated the release of her new album, *A Public Affair*. The album debuted at number five on the Billboard 200, and the single "A Public Affair" reached the top twenty of the Hot 100.

Jessica's second movie, *Employee of the Month*, hit theaters in October 2006, and soon thereafter she was shooting a third movie, *Blonde Ambition*, costarring Luke Wilson.

In addition, Jessica continued promoting Dessert Beauty, the line of edible beauty products she launched in April 2004; acting as a celebrity spokesperson for Proactiv (preventative acne skincare products); and fulfilling her duties as Operation Smile's International Youth Ambassador. She and her longtime friend and hairstylist, Ken Paves, launched a line of faux hair extensions on the Home Shopping Network in 2006. She was also reportedly working on a line of clothing, shoes, and handbags.

Since the divorce, gossip columnists have reported that Jessica has dated several of Hollywood's hottest guys, including Maroon 5's Adam Levine and Grammy Award-winning singer John Mayer. In fact, she joined Mayer on tour during his January 2007 concerts in Florida, singing and dancing to his music.

Jessica's career continues to flourish, with new opportunities and offers pouring in almost daily. In May 2007 it was announced that Jessica would star in a film called *Major Movie Star*, beating out Hollywood starlet Brittany Murphy for the role. The little Texas girl with big dreams has achieved many of those dreams already, but her fans know there is much more to come.

As Jessica reflects on the past few years and looks to the future, she has to smile. In fact, the southern girl with the sweet spirit says she has no regrets.

"I believe the best way to move on is to move on. I would go back and live my life exactly the same way. . . ."

CHRONOLOGY

1980	Jessica Ann Simpson is born on July 10 in Dallas, Texas
1992	Auditions unsuccessfully for *The All New Mickey Mouse Club*
1995	Graduates from Richardson North Junior High in Richardson, Texas
1998	Leaves J. J. Pearce High School in Richardson to promote her first album and later gets her GED. She meets Nick Lachey of the singing group 98 Degrees at the Hollywood Christmas Parade
1999	Releases her debut album, *Sweet Kisses*
2000	Wins two Teen Choice Awards for Breakout Artist and Love Song of the Year
2001	Releases her second album, *Irresistible*
2002	Gets engaged to Nick Lachey; they marry on October 26
2003	Jessica and Nick adjust to being married in front of millions of viewers on their MTV show *Newlyweds: Nick & Jessica*
2004	Launches an edible line of beauty products called Dessert Beauty. *The Jessica Simpson Show,* which is a pilot show for a sitcom on ABC, is filmed but is rejected by network executives in May
2005	Stars in *The Dukes of Hazzard* movie; *Newlyweds: Nick & Jessica* wins a People's Choice Award for Favorite Reality Show; travels to Kenya to work with Operation Smile. Jessica and Nick officially separate in November
2006	Jessica's album *A Public Affair* is released on August 29
2007	Jessica begins dating Grammy Award–winning singer John Mayer; she announces she will star in *Major Movie Star*

DISCOGRAPHY

Albums

2006	*A Public Affair*
2004	*Re-Joyce: The Christmas Album*
2003	*In This Skin*
2002	*This Is the Remix*
2001	*Irresistible*
1999	*Sweet Kisses*

Selected Hit Singles

2006	"A Public Affair"
2004	"Let It Snow, Let It Snow, Let It Snow"
2003	"Sweetest Sin"
	"Take My Breath Away"
2002	"Irresistible" (with Lil' Bow Wow—So So Def Remix)
2001	"Irresistible"
1999	"I Wanna Love You Forever"
	"Where You Are" (with Nick Lachey)
	"I Think I'm in Love with You"

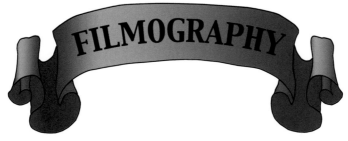

FILMOGRAPHY

2007	*Blonde Ambition*
2006	*Employee of the Month*
2005	*The Dukes of Hazzard*
2003–2005	*Newlyweds: Nick & Jessica* (TV series)
2003	*The Twilight Zone* (TV series—guest spot)

FURTHER READING

Books

Dougherty, Terri. *People in the News: Jessica Simpson and Nick Lachey.* San Diego, California: Lucent Books, 2005.

Kjelle, Marylou Morano. *Ashlee Simpson.* Hockessin, Delaware: Mitchell Lane Publishers, 2005.

Wheeler, Jill C. *Jessica Simpson.* Edina, Minnesota: Checkerboard Books, 2005.

Articles

AIM Pages: *Jessica Simpson – Six Degrees,* "A Message from Jessica" http://www.aimpages.com/js6degrees/profile.html

AllMoviePortal: "Jessica Simpson" http://www.allmovieportal.com/c/jessicasimpson.html

Ankeny, Jason. "Jessica Simpson Biography" http://www.starpulse.com/Music/Simpson,_Jessica/Biography/

The Bosh: "Nick Lachey Not Ready to Marry Vanessa Minnillo" January 14, 2007, http://thebosh.com/archives/2007/01/nick_lachey_not_ready_to_marry_vanessa_minnillo

Kidzworld: *Entertainment: Celebrity Vault,* "Jessica Simpson Biography" www.kidzworld.com/article/174-jessica-simpson-biography

LyricsFreak: "Jessica Simpson" http://www.lyricsfreak.com/j/jessica+simpson/biography.html

Works Consulted

Ambekar, Yogesh. "Jessica Simpson Biography" http://www.buzzle.com/editorials/1-20-2005-64533.asp

Celebrity Sizzle: *Jessica Simpson* http://www.celebritysizzle.com/JessicaSimpson

Celeb Source: "Jessica Simpson's African Epiphany"
http://www.celebsource.org/jessica-simpson/jessica-simpsons-african-epiphany/

Celeb Spin: "Jessica Simpson"
http://www.celebspin.com/jessica-simpson/

CNN: *Transcripts*, "CNN *Larry King Live:* Interview with Nick Lachey, Jessica Simpson" http://transcripts.cnn.com/TRANSCRIPTS/0310/14/lkl.00.html

Epic Records: *Jessica Simpson* http://www.jessicasimpson.com

Finan, Kristin. *Entertainment: Movies*, "Jessica Simpson Backs in to Short Shorts of Daisy Duke" http://www.jsonline.com/story/index.aspx?id=346173

IMDb: *Jessica Simpson* http://www.imdb.com/name/nm0005433/

Monsters and Critics: *People News*, "Jessica Simpson Rues Breakup" http://people.monstersandcritics.com/news/printer_1242861.php

Operation Smile: "Jessica Simpson Meets with Members of Congress," and "Jessica Simpson in Kenya" http://www.operationsmile.org/aboutus/spokespeople/jessica_simpson/

Sanchez, Robert. *News*, "Interview: Jessica Simpson"
http://www.moviehole.net/news/6048.html

Simpson, Jessica. *I Do: Achieving Your Dream Wedding*. Chicago: NVU Productions, 2003.

TV.com: "Jessica Simpson" http://www.tv.com/jessica-simpson/person/37589/trivia.html

Warech, Jon, and Stephen M. Silverman. *People News*, "Jessica Simpson Rocks Out at John Mayer Concert," January 29, 2007 http://www.people.com/people/article/0,,20010140,00.html

Web Addresses

Celebrity Wonder: *Jessica Simpson Picture, Profile, Gossip, and News* http://www.celebritywonder.com/html/jessicasimpson.html

Operation Smile http://www.operationsmile.org

INDEX